Life Death And Other Famous Recipes

Volume One

Bryan J Zimmerman

Life Death And Other Famous Recipes

Volume One

Photography, illustrations, and poetry from the somewhat
lucid imagination of Bryan J Zimmerman

Bryan J Zimmerman

Copyright © 2025 Bryan J Zimmerman

All rights reserved.

ISBN-13: 978-1419689482

ISBN-10: 1419689487

Foreword

A decade. Ten years of moments, memories, and milestones woven together to create the foundation of this book. What you now hold in your hands is a labor of love—born from quiet reflections, countless hours, and an unyielding pursuit of creative expression. This is the first of a two-volume journey, a testament to the ever-unfolding exploration of life and art.

Within these pages, poetry, photography, and illustrations intertwine—three distinct yet harmonious mediums working together to capture life's fleeting nuances. Each poem, image, and illustration is an invitation to feel, to question, and to find solace. This collection is not here to provide answers but to spark curiosity, guiding you into the intimate spaces where art and emotion converge.

To those encountering my work for the first time, welcome. And to the many who have walked alongside me on this creative journey, I am deeply grateful for your steadfast support and encouragement. Art is rarely created in isolation, and this book reflects the countless inspirations drawn from the people, places, and moments that have shaped my path.

I owe special thanks to my wife, Donna, for her unwavering love and belief in me, and to my children, Jami, Julian, and Wendy, for their encouragement and faith in this vision. Your support has been my foundation, and I am endlessly grateful. To my brother, Erik, whose photographic talent helped elevate my own, thank you for inspiring me to see the world through a sharper lens.

In loving memory of my daughter Jami, whom we lost in 2017, I humbly ask for donations to an equestrian charity of your choice. Horses were her passion, and this small tribute allows her love for them to ripple outward, touching others in the way she touched all of us. May her spirit, so full of kindness and joy, linger in the hearts of those who read these pages.

Whether you've come to pause, to reflect, or to seek comfort, I hope this book offers a moment of connection and discovery. In a world often clouded by uncertainty, may these pages remind you of the quiet power of art to unite us, to heal, and to inspire.

Thank you for being here.

Bryan J Zimmerman

CONTENTS

Taken Too Soon	1
The Angel's Weep	4
Nine-Seven	5
Black	8
Ode to Judas	9
Home	12
The Truth	13
Alone	16
The Touch of an Angel	17
The Funeral	20
Scream	21
Whore	24
About the author	26
Photography	28

Bryan J Zimmerman

Taken Too Soon

To my beautiful daughter, Jami
1986-2017

I see you,
In the drops of rain and dancing leaves,
In the moonlit silhouette caressing the trees,
And the horses grazing in the field.

I feel you,
In the stillness of a quiet room,
The gentle, unseen wind,
As I dream, you linger unseen,
Nestled within my tears.

I love you,
For your smile and laughter,
Your compassion and resilience,
And giving unconditionally.

I long for,
One more ribbon,
One more show,
And the warmth of one last hug.

For you are,
Forever in my heart,
Always in my thoughts,

And only a memory away from a wink, and smile.

Life, Death, and Other Famous Recipes - Vol 1

The Angels Weep

Dedicated to my soul sister, Michelle

Trapped beneath the ice,
Darkness taunting my sanity.
So cold is the poison
Of guilt, pain, and regret.

This prison surrounds me,
Built not with stone,
But with torment
And memories that haunt.

My tears
Dance on the edge of death's razor,
Feeding rage,
Twisting my mind.

I seek Heaven
Only to feed my demons,
I make my bed in Hell
Only to lie with the cherubs.

I cry out to God,
But the silence deafens,
Leaving me to my own purgatory,
Wondering why you went away.

I stare through the window,
Drifting into sleep.
Is it rain I hear falling,
Or do the angels weep?

Nine - Seven

On the last eve of the full moon,
As I watched the mist dance upon the mountains,
And the moon caress the treetops,
My eyes closed,
And I slipped into a dream.

I dreamt of your beauty,
Standing at the edge of our castle,
Awaiting my return from a long journey.

I see you in the distance.

Upon my descent, your beauty grows more vivid—
Hair flowing like untamed oceans,
Eyes brimming with love,
Your gown, cascading like whispers of the Fae.

A hint of jasmine fills the air.

The thought of our lips meeting
Is a vision fit only for angels.

We will lie among the lilies,
Making love beneath the star-filled sky.
Our gazes, locked upon one another,
Speak all the words unspoken.

I shall caress thee with a dove's feather
And bathe you with petals of rose and lilac.
For you are my princess, and I, your prince—
I cannot imagine myself with another.

True beauty is found deep within the soul,
But true love, I have only found in you.

You will always hold a piece of my heart, a part of my soul,
In this life and beyond.

Life, Death, and Other Famous Recipes - Vol 1

Black

Faceless demons
Play upon your soul
Like a fine-tuned piano.

Whispering,
Taunting,
A haunting melody,
An orchestral nightmare.

You extend your aging hands,
Only to find death,
Seething blackness,
Dark pit,
Endless night.

Dragon's breath
Upon your neck,
Welcome to the feast.

You cannot cry out,
There is no turning back,
There is no tomorrow,
For your plate is full
Of yesterday's failures.

Hollow moon,
The sun a corpse,
Choke on a piece of guilt,
Drink deep from the sea of despair.

Sop up your dreams
With a slice of hatred,
Let your bones digest
What is left
Of happiness.

And then you see,
Your ship has arrived,
But the captain is dead,
For he has seen your future.

Ode to Judas

This cannot be,
A dream, perhaps?
For a murderer, I am not!

Selfish thoughts,
Greed...

No!

This is not happening.
Have I sentenced a god to die?

Leave me,
Hosts of evil!
Your mockery
Boils my blood.

It must end
Here,
Now.

That tree,
My tomb.

Forgive me,
I have sinned.

Hell awaits.
My fate has been sealed.

Life, Death, and Other Famous Recipes - Vol 1

Bryan J Zimmerman

Home

In the early morning hour,
Soft sand beneath my feet,
Clouds overhead,
Seagulls sing their love song.

On the horizon,
The sun splashes the sea with vibrant colors,
Hand-painted by the Goddess.

The sweet smell of salt exhilarates my senses,
Cool breeze heals,
The waters lay their treasures at my feet,
Once filled with life,
Now empty graves for our taking.

I am home here,
One with the ocean,
Her gift to the soul.

We have our fill of love,
On the sand,
We are one, a blessed union.
You are my lover,
You are my friend,
You are my ocean breeze.

The Truth

Chained to the wall of destiny,
Shackled by despair.

A fallen star,
A gaping hole left in the twilight.
My days are blackened, my soul parched.

I am both prisoner and warden,
With no key.

Chasing the truth,
Like a dog chasing its tail.

And like the dog,
My chase ends in despair.

My soul burns with fire,
Hatred bleeds from my blinded eyes.

I seek the child within,
Abused and beaten.

Must he still serve his sentence?

Life, Death, and Other Famous Recipes - Vol 1

Alone

I long to be hidden
from this world's darkness,
far from judgmental eyes,
in my private cocoon.

Leave me
to ponder,
to pray.

Alone.

You'll never understand me,
my thoughts,
or who I am, who I was.
Only one understands.

Please go away,
brainwashed scum,
A shadow I can't escape.
Just leave me.
Let silence be my only company.

Alone.

How I long to be alone,
behind safe walls,
my fortress, my castle,
preparing for battle
as demons gather for war.

Please go,
return to your perfect world.
This prison is full; no more room.

Please go, for I long only to be
Alone.

The Touch of an Angel

Hands upon my flesh,
Angels' breath,
One touch—
An eternal bond
Between the souls of strangers.

Erotic,
Spiritual.

I can almost taste the heavens,
As your warm magic
Courses through my body.

If you listen closely,
You can hear my heart,
Trembling with the melodies of my passion.
All hurt and sorrow are lifted,
My worries, nothing more than a memory.

My entire being basks in this moment,
My soul longs to stay,
Just a moment longer.

As we part ways,
And the veil of reality is lifted,
Know that your touch invokes jealousy among the gods,
And envy amid the angels.

Life, Death, and Other Famous Recipes - Vol 1

The Funeral

The fire within my heart,
Cold to the touch.

My dreams, they taunt me—
Lucid tales of my life,
Blood-red.

My twisted heart screams for passion;
It bleeds loneliness,
Pulsating to the beat of a death drum.

Take this living corpse,
Bury it near the river,
Where spirits dance, water flows,
And fear is nothing more than a word.

For this coffin—my prison—is not my own;
It belongs to another.
Remove the nails, undo the shackles,
Breathe life,
That I may live again.

Scream

The day was dark,
A mist covered the sky.
Thinking of what was to come,
My thoughts were but a lie.

As I looked ahead,
I slipped into a dream.
Before I could awake,
I heard my body scream.

Then came the thunder—
I felt my heartbeat stop.
Dark turned to black,
And the ground, so hot.

As I came to life,
I turned to look around.
My mind felt numb;
Ice covered the ground.

When I finally gathered
What had taken place,
My body thrown into the cold,
I wiped the ice from my face.

Looking on in horror,
My eyes fixed on the ground.
What meant the most to me
Lay broken in the mist,
Unable to make a sound.

I began to panic,
Running toward the grass.
My body felt so numb,
Awareness fading fast.

To this very day,
It feels like just a dream—
That cold, dark, misty morning,
The day I had to scream.

Life, Death, and Other Famous Recipes - Vol 1

Bryan J Zimmerman

Whore

We are deranged puppets,
Bloodied strings tangled on decaying thorns.
We slit our wrists on empty prayers,
To feed the whore with tainted blood.

Seek and you shall find her,
Legs spread wide,
No fee, only consequence

Her umbilical cord is a snake, feeding on abandoned souls
Reducing their dreams to ash.

In her world,
Angels dance with corpses,
And heaven vomits up fallen stars.
The night quivers in her presence.

Discarded fetus,
Lost in the back alley of our nightmares,
Crawling among the bones of its forefathers,
As hypocrisy drips from the stones.

On the horizon,
The sun slowly pools into a lake of bile,
The moon struggles to lift herself from the pervasive slime.

Black rain begins to fall.

Fucking slaves!
The truth is sewage to your nostrils,
Like swine to the trough,
you feed happily on political vomit
Choking on the phlegm of your filthy lies.

Our mouths have been sewn shut,
And the whore has removed our eyes.

Will no one stand up for us?

Bryan J Zimmerman

About the Author

A celebrated poet, author, and professional musician, Bryan was born and raised in Northeast Pennsylvania and now resides in South Florida, with a career spanning decades of creative exploration. Rooted in both the written word and the performing arts, he draws from a lifetime of experiences, blending vivid imagery, heartfelt emotion, and a deep appreciation for life's intricacies into his work.

An avid storyteller, Bryan finds inspiration in the natural world, the subtleties of human connection, and the quiet, unspoken moments that often go unnoticed. His background as a photographer further enriches his artistry, enabling him to capture life's fleeting beauty through a visual lens that complements his literary voice.

In addition to his literary achievements, Bryan has spent years captivating audiences as a guitarist with Lehigh Valley rock band Dirty Blond. His dual passion for music and literature is evident in his writing, where rhythm and lyricism intertwine seamlessly throughout his poetry and prose.

This book represents the culmination of a decade-long journey, offering readers an intimate glimpse into Bryan's world of poetry, illustrations, and photography.

When not immersed in his creative pursuits, Bryan cherishes time with his miniature schnauzer, Gemma, exploring new technology, and finding serenity in the harmony of nature and the divine feminine.

To explore Bryan's music and photography,
please scan the QR code below

www.ingramcontent.com/pod-product-compliance
Lightning Source LLC
LaVergne TN
LVHW070046070526
838200LV00028B/403